JUDAISM
FOR BEGINNERS

CHARLES SZLAKMANN

Writers and Readers

I wish to thank Professor A. Derczansky, Head
of Research at CNRS, for his support and help
with this book.

WRITERS AND READERS PUBLISHING, INC.
P.O. Box 461, Village Station
New York, New York 10014

ISBN 0 86316 101 4
1 2 3 4 5 6 7 8 9 0

Manufactured in the United States of America

Glossary

Ashkenazy: Denotes Jews of central and eastern European origin.

Bar Mitzvah: Religious maturity for men, attained at the age of thirteen.

Bris Mila: Circumcision.

Kabbala: mystical commentary on the Torah.

Kosher: Denotes food fit for consumption, i.e., which conforms to the religious prescriptions.

Shofar: Ram's horn. Sounded during the services for the New Year and the Day of Atonement.

Golah: Exile.

Hasidism: Movement which places the accent on joy in the ritual practices and stresses the mystical aspects of Judaism.

Messiah: Man descended from the royal house of David who will establish the Kingdom of God on earth.

Midrash: Interpretation of the Torah.

Mitzvah: Religious commandment.

Sephardic: Denotes Jews of Mediterranean origin.

Talmud: Collection of the commentaries and interpretations of Oral Law, itself a commentary on the Bible.

Teshuvah: Return (to oneself; to God). Repentance. Response.

Torah: In the narrowest sense, the five Books of Moses; in the broader sense, all the holy books of Judaism.

Yeshivah: School specializing in Torah study.

HOW TO READ THIS BOOK?

FIRST, A LITTLE HISTORY...

א ... <u>Up to the emancipation</u>
<u>(18th Century). Page 6:</u>
The first Jew. Egypt. Jewish
Kingdoms and prophets. The Exile, etc.

ב <u>God and Man. Page 34:</u>
God is one. God the Living, God the
Creator, God the Just and God the Merciful.
Man and his dual instincts. Self-discipline! etc.

ג <u>The Torah. Page 52:</u>
There are two: the oral and
the written. (Both should be
studied.) Talmud, etc.

ד <u>Jewish Ethics. Jewish Society. Page 70:</u>
The dignity of work. Ownership and
slavery... the symbolic meaning of the
pierced ear. The "haves" and "have nots."

The Jewish People: From Abraham to the Emancipation

According to Jewish tradition the history of Israel started with just one man, Abraham. He was the first to proclaim the principles of monotheism (c. 1700 B.C.) despite opposition from a hostile environment (Chaldea).

Tradition had it that God formed a special alliance with Abraham.

The Covenant

"I SHALL FORM AN ETERNAL COVENANT BETWEEN MYSELF, YOU AND YOUR DESCENDANTS."

The Ideal of Justice

"ALL YOU HAVE TO DO IN RETURN IS TO FOLLOW THE PATH OF THE ETERNAL FATHER WITH VIRTUE AND JUSTICE."

Universalism

"ALL THE NATIONS OF THE EARTH SHALL REJOICE IN YOU."

The Exile

"YOUR DESCENDANTS SHALL BE EXILED TO A STRANGE LAND WHERE THEY SHALL BE ENSLAVED AND OPPRESSED ...."

The Promised Land

"IT IS TO YOU AND YOUR DESCEN- -DANTS THAT I GIVE THIS LAND."

AS FOR ME – WHAT AM I – BUT ASHES AND DUST?

THIS IS A HEAVY BURDEN FOR ME TO BEAR!

Abraham had two sons

ONE BORN OF SARAH

ISAAC

THE OTHER OF HAGAR

AND ISHMAEL – ANCESTOR OF THE ARABS.

BORN IN THE PROMISED LAND

CONFLICT OF HERITAGE

LINEAGE OF THE JEWISH PEOPLE

7

– Isaac had two sons, born of Rebecca.

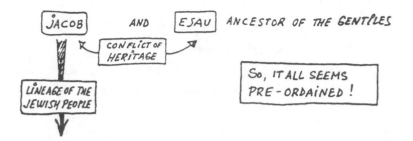

Jacob had 12 sons (his children by Rachel and Leah), who are the ancestors of the 12 tribes of Israel.

The Jews emigrated to Egypt, driven by famine. In the beginning the living conditions were extremely favorable, but then a series of political upheavals took place. Reduced to slavery, the Jews were soon threatened with extermination.

But God did not abandon the Jewish people.

Led by Moses, a Hebrew brought up at the court of Pharaoh, the Jews left Egypt, helped by a series of miracles.

This is the **Exodus** (c. 1500 B.C.), that marks the entry of the Jewish people into history.

9

After the flight from Egypt Moses led the Jews into the desert, to the foot of Mount Sinai. There God gave the Jewish people the Torah and the Ten Commandments.

After wandering in the desert for 40 years the Jewish people reached the promised land, gaining it by conquest. At first they organized themselves into a federation, then into a kingdom, the high point of which was reached with the reign of Solomon (c. 1000 B.C.). The first Temple at Jerusalem was built under Solomon; it was said that 'God Himself was present in the Temple.'

But with the death of Solomon, a split occurred (c. 933): two rival kingdoms rose up from the remains of the old kingdom.

The two kingdoms gradually abandoned the teachings of the Torah, preferring instead to practice idolatry and sinking into the mire of corruption. They waged war incessantly, until their ultimate destruction (final for the kingdom Israel, temporary for the kingdom of Judea).

This period (the split, destruction and restoration of Judea) is the **era of the great prophets,** who derived their inspiration directly from God. The prophets were not simply instruments of God, but had the specific task of warning their contemporaries of the terrible disasters which were imminent if they persisted in their wicked ways.

The prophets demanded total submission to the ideals of the Torah, stressing in particular two requirements: it is not enough merely to perform the ritual. God demands the highest moral standards in human relationships coupled with social justice.

After having long prophesied the fall of the Jewish kingdoms, the prophets announced their great vision of the rebirth of Israel, the dawning of the messianic age, the age of justice and lasting peace for all humanity.

"And nation shall not lift up sword against nation. . . . "

On their return from the Babylonian exile (536 B.C.) the Jews rebuilt the temple of Jerusalem, regained their independence from the Greeks and the Syrians and restored the kingdom of Judea. Ultimately, however, the Jewish state succumbed to the might of the Roman Empire, despite fierce resistance (last revolt = 135 AD).

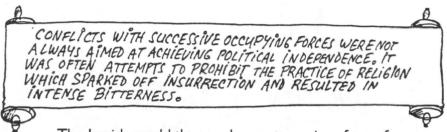

CONFLICTS WITH SUCCESSIVE OCCUPYING FORCES WERE NOT ALWAYS AIMED AT ACHIEVING POLITICAL INDEPENDENCE. IT WAS OFTEN ATTEMPTS TO PROHIBIT THE PRACTICE OF RELIGION WHICH SPARKED OFF INSURRECTION AND RESULTED IN INTENSE BITTERNESS.

The Jewish world then underwent a series of transformations, which, to a large extent, determined the face of Judaism today:

The Jewish people lost all sovereignty for two thousand years . . . **and became a scattered nation.**

"IF I FORGET YOU, JERUSALEM, MAY MY RIGHT HAND LOSE ITS CUNNING.."

IN FACT, THE PROCESS OF DISPERSAL HAD STARTED WELL BEFORE, MANY PEOPLE EMIGRATING OF THEIR OWN FREE WILL. HOWEVER, WITH THE ROMAN OCCUPATION, PALESTINE GRADUALLY LOST ITS JEWISH INHABITANTS, UNTIL ONLY A TINY MINORITY REMAINED.

Pharisees and Sadducees

Two rival factions confronted in Jerusalem before the destruction of the Temple.

The Sadducees   and the Pharisees

The Sadducees:

These were the priests attached to the Temple. They were extremely unpopular and disappeared along with the Temple.

The Pharisees:

Close to the People, the Pharisees gave Judaism the face we still know today:
—the essential role of the Rabbis as teachers and interpreters of the Torah.
—the importance of the Synagogue as a place for the teaching of the Torah.

With the destruction of the Temple, the people scattered and the Judaism of the Pharisees became adapted to the new conditions.

Birth of the Talmud

It was forbidden to consign oral law to the written word: however, in the light of the problems posed by the Jewish dispersal, the Rabbis of Palestine, under the leadership of Rabbi Judah the Prince, decided to write down one part, in the 3rd century AD; this first work is called the *Mishnah* (teachings). (See page 60.)

The *Mishnah* itself gave rise to a number of commentaries, which are collectively known as the *Gemara*.

The two (*Mishnah* and *Gemara*) were themselves collected together and given the name

Talmud (study),

which became the corner-stone of Jewish life for the coming centuries

The Great Exile (up to the 18th century). Each period of history saw the emergence of several great Jewish centers, which migrated from place to place, depending on the degree of persecution.

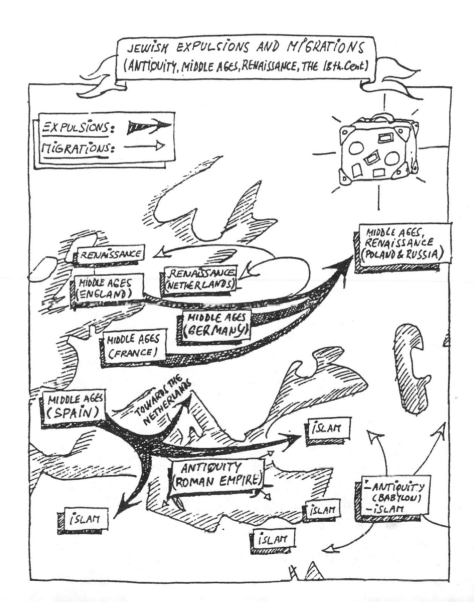

JEWISH EXPULSIONS AND MIGRATIONS
(ANTIQUITY, MIDDLE AGES, RENAISSANCE, THE 18th.Cent.)

EXPULSIONS:
MIGRATIONS:

RENAISSANCE

MIDDLE AGES
(ENGLAND)

RENAISSANCE
(NETHERLANDS)

MIDDLE AGES
(GERMANY)

MIDDLE AGES
(FRANCE)

MIDDLE AGES,
RENAISSANCE
(POLAND & RUSSIA)

MIDDLE AGES
(SPAIN)

TOWARDS THE
NETHERLANDS

ISLAM

ANTIQUITY
(ROMAN EMPIRE)

ISLAM

-ANTIQUITY
(BABYLON)
-ISLAM

ISLAM

ISLAM

■ Two great centers of the past: the Roman Empire and Babylon

Favorable conditions . . .

—in Babylon, the Jews enjoyed almost complete political and religious autonomy under their leader, the "Exilarch!" Intellectual activity flourished (many of the Talmudic commentaries were written during this period).

—under the Roman Empire, the Jews were granted citizenship and were represented in all classes of society. The practice of Judaism proved to have powerful attractions, and there were many converts despite opposition from intellectual quarters.

The climate gradually changed with the triumph of Christianity.

■ Jews in Christian lands

In general terms, it is under the "shadow of the cross" that the Jews have suffered their most tragic turns of fate (extermination in the Middle Ages, expulsion from Spain, the genocide of 1939-45).

At the root of the "doctrine of hate" is a conflict of heritage.

This ideological rivalry was exacerbated by the success of Jewish proselytizing and led to the imposition of restrictions by the Church:

The Jews thus existed in the few areas of tolerance offered by Christian society, and in this they were not entirely unsuccessful. They played a significant role in the development of commercial and banking activities, at least up until the time of the Crusades. This adaptation was enhanced by the aspirations of the Jewish communities themselves.

**The Crusades encouraged the habit of
anti-Semitic violence (first Crusade: 1069).**

COUNTLESS COMMUNITIES ALL OVER EUROPE WERE THUS EXTERMINATED BY THE CRUSADERS, PARTICULARLY IN THE RHINE VALLEY, A ROUTE FAVOURED...

BY THOSE GOING TO FIGHT THE INFIDEL. THE JEWS OFTEN CHOSE DEATH, PREFERRING BURNING TO BAPTISM.

Conclusion

After the massacres and restrictive measures the countries of western Europe expelled their Jewish communities:

Expulsion from England: 1290   from Germany: 1350-60
from France: 1394   from Spain: 1492

The deadly violence was frequently perpetrated by the lower ranks of the clergy, local potentates and unruly rabble. The higher authorities sometimes played a moderating role:
—the Jews were given refuge in the papal states.
—the Church even developed the theory of the "nation of witnesses."

IF THEY HAVE FALLEN FROM GRACE, IT IS BECAUSE GOD IS PUNISHING THEM FOR NOT RECOGNIZING CHRIST.

GOD DOES NOT WANT THE JEWS EXTERMINATED, BUT THEY SHALL WANDER THE EARTH "TO BEAR WITNESS TO THE ERROR OF THEIR WAYS."

25

The golden Judeo-Hispanic age . . .

Under Islamic rule the Jews enjoyed particularly fortunate times. At the start of the process of Christian "reconquest," they maintained their position. This was the golden age, when Jews were often highly placed.

This was the Judeo-Hispanic era, which saw the development of the *Kabbala*—an esoteric commentary on the Bible. In the 13th century a Spanish Jew called Moses de León published the *Zohar*, a major Kabbalistic work. To an extent, he offered consolation to the European communities in the midst of the massacres and expulsions, allowing them to catch a glimpse of the final liberation.

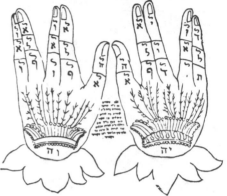

But with the Christian reconquest . . .

YES, LET'S ACCEPT OFFICIALLY... AND IN SECRET WE'LL CARRY ON PRACTISING THE RELIGION OF OUR FOREFATHERS....

MARRANOS

Having accepted baptism for the most part, the Jews saved their own lives and even returned to their former positions of power (in 1484 a Jew was Chancellor of the Spanish Royal Exchequer).

... the expulsion (1492) and anti-Semitic racial discrimination followed.

THESE JEWS ARE CHRISTIANS IN PUBLIC, BUT STILL JEWS AT HOME!

THE TRIBUNAL OF THE HOLY INQUISITION WILL SOON ROOT OUT THE JEW HIDING WITHIN THE CHRISTIAN!

BURN THEM.... BURN THE JEWS!

A TRUE CHRISTIAN HAS ONLY TO PROVE THE PURITY OF HIS BLOOD!

The Inquisition put one-third (approx. 300,000) of the *Marranos* to death at the stake in the *autos-da-fé* (acts of faith). And in 1492 the Jews were expelled from Spain.

From a golden age to a dark age: Poland and Russia

Called to Poland in the Middle Ages by kings who wanted to establish a commercial and financial infrastructure, the Jews, who had been hounded from other parts of western Europe, settled there. In the beginning they enjoyed civil and religious autonomy and great material prosperity. But with the increasing loss of Polish independence, the Jews once again found themselves in their familiar role of scapegoats.

For communities which had flourished in earlier times, the hour of suffering had come:

—material descent into poverty;

—virulent anti-Semitism to an extent hitherto unknown, practiced by the state, population and clergy of both Russian Orthodox and Polish Catholic Churches.

During these dark times there emerged from the depths of Russian/Polish Judaism a new movement: Hasidism. In western Europe the Jews lived in small villages inhabited almost exclusively by Jews: the *shtetl*. Religious (and later political) life was extraordinarily intense. From these origins grew a movement which was to renew and revitalize Judaism.

Hasidism became an immensely popular movement—and still is today—which offered the mass of disinherited Jews of western Europe a point of focus in a time of dislocation.

Jews under Islamic rule

The lot of Jews under Islam was infinitely preferable to that of those under the shadow of the cross. But there were certainly times when they were the victims of outbursts of fanaticism and subject to restrictive measures.

- SINCE THE JEWS AND THE CHRISTIANS ARE "PEOPLES OF THE BOOK"
- SINCE WE ALSO REVERE THE GREAT PROPHETS ABRAHAM, MOSES, JESUS... ... AND MOHAMMED, JEWS AND CHRISTIANS WILL BE "DHIMMIS" (PROTECTED)! THIS MEANS:
- SPECIAL LIVING QUARTERS
- SPECIAL GARMENTS
- THEY SHALL NOT BEAR ARMS
- ETC.

OF COURSE, THE PROTECTION COULD BE IMPROVED UPON... BUT AT LEAST OUR LAW IS QUITE CLEAR.

"The Jew is more despised than hated." (Poliakov)
There was even a form a off Judeo-Arabian symbiosis" that culminated in medieval Spain, where the Jews often held influential positions as diplomats, doctors, financiers etc.

THIS SYMBIOSIS PLAYED AN IMPORTANT PART IN THE EVOLUTION OF THE WESTERN CULTURE:

GREEK PHILOSOPHERS UNKNOWN IN THE WEST... ΘΣ ν πεια

DISCOVERED AND TRANSLATED BY THE ARAB ...

...TRANSLATED INTO HEBREW...

... THEN INTO LATIN; FOLLOWED BY DISCOVERY OF THESE TEXTS BY THE WEST: THE 'RENAISSANCE'

This was the "golden Judeo-Arabian age," which gave birth to Jewish philosophy.

ALL OUR BELIEFS CAN BE UPHELD BY PHILOSOPHICAL SPECULATION!

APART FROM WHICH, THIS FASHIONABLE ARISTOTELIAN PHILOSOPHY IS PLAYING HAVOC WITH US JEWS!

WELL, THERE'S ONLY ONE THING TO DO, AND THAT'S TO WRITE THE "GUIDE TO THE PERPLEXED" (MAIMONIDES).

Maimonides, the "eagle of the synagogue," is the author of another work of great genius, which is a systematic examination of Talmudic legislation—the "strong hand."

TOWARDS THE MIDDLE OF THE 17th CENTURY, THE WHOLE OF THE JEWISH WORLD WAS SHAKEN BY AN EXTRAORDINARY MOVEMENT:

THE MESSIAH HAS COME !!!

LET US GO TO THE HOLY LAND !!

INCREDIBLE - ALL THE JEWS ARE FOLLOWING HIM !!!

BUT THE SULTAN, RULER OF THE HOLY LAND, FORCED SHABBETAI Z'VI TO CONVERT TO ISLAM, ON PAIN OF DEATH. HAVING ENGENDERED SUCH HOPE, SHABBETAI Z'VI MAINTAINED SOME DISCIPLES EVEN AFTER HIS CONVERSION, AND HAD SOME INFLUENCE ON THE SUBSEQUENT EVOLUTION OF JUDAISM.

Ashkenazim and Sephardim
During the 18th century the Jewish world gave birth to two distinctly different cultures:

Sephardim
which means "Spain." This term extends to all the Jews of the Mediterranean basin.

Ashkenazim
which means "Germany." This term extends to all the Jews of western, central and eastern Europe and the US.

DO YOU SPEAK LADINO? THE LANGUAGE PECULIAR TO JEWS OF SPANISH... AND JUDEO-ARAB ORIGIN.

DO YOU SPEAK YIDDISH? IT'S A MIXTURE OF HEBREW AND MEDIEVAL GERMAN.

THE MELODIES OF OUR PRAYERS ARE NOT LIKE YOURS. WE LIKE ORIENTA-A-A-A-A-AL MUSIC!

OUR WEAKNESS IS SOULFUL, SLAVIC MELODIES (...JUST THE MELODIES).

HAVE YOU EVER HEARD OF COUSCOUS?

HAVE YOU EVER HEARD OF GEFILTE FISH?

But there is no question of two separate peoples:
—the Torah remains the same.
—one single code of law, the "laid table," has been accepted throughout Judaism since the 16th century. This code is still observed today.
—intellectual exchanges are frequent;
—geographic migrations equally so.

 **God and Man**

—God, master of the universe.
—Man, master of the earth, privileged partner of God.

God is One

The birth of Jewish people is closely linked to the ideology of monotheism. Abraham was the first Jew because according to Jewish tradition he was the first to proclaim the principles of monotheism.

BUT, WHAT IS GOD ?!?!? ???

THE TEXTS DO NOT DEAL WITH THIS QUESTION: THE ESSENCE OF GOD IS SAID TO BE BEYOND THE COMPREHENSION OF MAN.

GOD IS A PRE-EMINENT BEING.

WE DO NOT KNOW HOW TO PRONOUNCE THE FOUR LETTERS OF THE TETRAGRAMATRON WHICH FORMS THE NAME OF THE LORD

ANY REPRESENTATION OF GOD IN WHATEVER FORM (PICTURE OR STATUE) IS STRICTLY FORBIDDEN AND CONSIDERED TO BE IDOLATRY.

The commentary asks:

—Why does the Bible start with the letter *Bet*—the second letter of the alphabet? Why doesn't it start with the first letter, *Aleph*— a symbol of the oneness of God?

—One of the replies given is as follows: examine the shape of the *Bet* ב

(remember that Hebrew is read from right to left).

DO NOT SEEK TO KNOW WHAT IS ABOVE YOU!

THE ONLY OPENING IN THE LETTER "BET" IS AT THE FRONT. THUS..

GO FORWARD!

DO NOT SEEK TO KNOW WHAT IS BEFORE YOU!

In this way, Judaism proclaims **primacy of action.** This is why Jewish texts concentrate on religious and moral guidelines rather than on theological discussions.

DO NOT SEEK TO KNOW WHAT IS BELOW YOU!

God can be approached only through His relationship with the world.

God is not an abstract principle; God is a living, active being, with a personality of His own. . . .
What does God do?

 God is the creator of the universe, which was created from nothing.

Because God never "sits back" to contemplate His creation.

He intervenes constantly, and this intervention is not merely arbitrary: it has a **moral** meaning.

Thus, in Judaism there is no chance, no fatalism. God is just: "He punishes and rewards."

In Judaism, it is action which is the the most important

because . . .

The universe has a purpose . . .
To allow man to improve himself, to enhance creation by his own actions, by practicing virtue and justice. Judaism challenges the theory of the contradiction between "faith" and "action"—action being the logical outcome of faith.

In this way, man plays a central part:
he is God's privileged partner.

The two faces of Man:

Jewish tradition postulates the **clear distinction between good and evil.**

If man feels any aspiration towards goodness and justice, he is **unaware of its form.**

This form is defined by God.

It is given in the Torah—the repository of the divine word and eternal guide to man in his search for morality.

THE TABLETS OF THE LAW WERE MADE OF STONE - A SYMBOL OF ETERNITY BECAUSE ....

IN JUDAISM MORAL LAW NEVER CHANGES...

MOUNT SINAI IS IN A DESERT. DESERT: A PLACE FAR FROM CIVILIZATION. THE LAW APPLIES TO EVERYONE EQUALLY, WHEREVER THEY MAY BE!

IT IS MAN WHO MUST CHANGE!

In fact, Judaism challenges a morality created by human beings alone. Of necessity, this would be imperfect. The product of a given moment and place.

... TO DO GOOD ... TO DO EVIL ... IN ANY CASE, MAN CANNOT BE SAVED THROUGH HIS DEEDS, BUT THROUGH GOD....

...FROM WHOM HIS FAITH SPRINGS!

MAN IS NOT FREE!

NO, LUTHER!

JUDAISM DOES NOT AGREE!

EVERYTHING IS IN THE HANDS OF THE ALMIGHTY - EXCEPT FEAR OF THE ALMIGHTY!

BECAUSE MAN HAS BEEN GIVEN FREE WILL!

SZLAK MANU

43

Man has been given free will:
He has been given the capacity to choose good or evil, as defined in the Torah.

Being free, man carries total **responsibility for his actions** and will have to give an account of himself before his Creator when his time comes.

So, just as it is impossible to "trespass against the laws of nature without suffering the consequences," it is also quite impossible to "trespass against the moral code without suffering the penalties." "Punishment is equally inevitable in the latter, as in the former case." (Meyer Waxman)
This idea is fundamental to Jewish law.

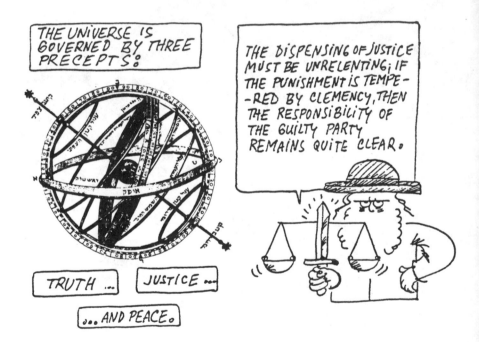

THE UNIVERSE IS GOVERNED BY THREE PRECEPTS:

THE DISPENSING OF JUSTICE MUST BE UNRELENTING; IF THE PUNISHMENT IS TEMPERED BY CLEMENCY, THEN THE RESPONSIBILITY OF THE GUILTY PARTY REMAINS QUITE CLEAR.

TRUTH ... JUSTICE ...

... AND PEACE.

There is, therefore, a link between the preservation of these values and a well-ordered world.

According to tradition, free will is given
to man **at the age of 13.** This
attainment of the state of religious
maturity . . .

. . . is marked by the ceremony of the
Bar Mitzvah, at which a young man puts on his phylacteries
(*tefilin*)—see "Rituals," p. 131—a symbol of the commandment which he will henceforth have to observe. The young
man is also called up to chant a passage of the Torah.

The very essence of human life is man's desperate struggle against his own evil inclinations, a struggle which can never be completed.

"THE WORLD WE INHABIT IS A CORRIDOR TO THE WORLD BEYOND" PREPARE YOURSELF IN THE CORRIDOR BY DOING GOOD DEEDS TO ENTER HIS PRESENCE...

אֵתֶם מְכוֹת "רַבְּי עֲקִיבָא"
מַן שֶׁבְּלְמַנֶה
שֶׁהֵבִיא הַקְנֶה

THIS IS WHY MAN IS SUPERIOR TO THE ANGELS:

THE ANGELS, WHO HAVE NO SUBSTANCE, ARE DEVOID OF EVIL INSTINCTS. THEY DO NOT HAVE TO FIGHT THEIR OWN NATURE TO ACCOMPLISH GOOD!

NO BUT...

THAT IS WHY ANGELS DO NOT HAVE FREE WILL. THEY HAVE NO NEED OF IT, SINCE THEY ACCOMPLISH ONLY THE WILL OF GOD.

MAN, ON THE OTHER HAND, MUST MAKE EFFORTS - OFTEN CONSI--DERABLE-TO CHOOSE BETWEEN GOOD AND EVIL- ALL THE MORE PRAISEWORTHY !!!

The greater a man's capacity for good—the greater his capacity for evil.

Judaism does not encourage mortification.

It is a question of disciplining the character and working for the general good:

". . . and you shall love God with both your hearts!"

Example:

Punishment and retribution

In the same way that the physical world is subject to strict laws, in the moral world also any action is either punished or rewarded. According to tradition, God has chosen the first day of the Jewish New Year—*Rosh Hashanah*—as the day on which the "souls of all living things" are examined and the "day of reckoning of all creatures" is determined.

In the physical world, such retribution is compulsory. In the moral world, however, **transgression does not bring immediate punishment: God expects—or hopes—that the sinner will repent and change his behavior.**

Repentance

In Hebrew, the word *teshuvah* means return (i.e., to God). This consists of examining the conscience and subsequent sincere repentance of any transgressions committed.

For repentance to "count," in order for God to "pass from the throne of justice to the throne of mercy," **any behavior which is found wanting must be rectified.**

According to tradition, there is particularly favorable time for repentance: this is the "ten days of *Teshuvah*," which begins on the first day of the New Year and ends on the tenth day, which is *Yom Kippur*, or the Day of Atonement.

On this day, the *shofar* (ram's horn) is sounded, as a plea to God for forgiveness, since He "abhors not the sinner but the sin" (See Festivals, p.115).

Teshuvah should be practiced all the time, however.

The commentaries deal with this problem at length.

1. What happens to us in this world is beyond human comprehension: we are ignorant of the quirks of Providence. All that we can be sure of is that good will triumph in the final reckoning.

2. God imposes additional trials on the good:
it is "suffering for love" which enables the good to strengthen their selfless faith.

3. Punishment and reward cannot be applied in this world alone. When a man dies, his soul comes before his creator and the celestial court will weigh his soul in the balance. Reward and punishment depend on the outcome. But the ideal is to serve God unselfishly.

 # The Torah

This is the collected holy writings of Judaism and related commentaries, which evolved over many centuries.

The word itself means:

> at
> the
> same
> time

—**teaching**—i.e., an account of Jewish understanding of the world, of man and his history.

—**instruction**—i.e., precise details of the principles by which man should be guided in his relations with his fellow men and with God.

The Torah was given by God to the Jewish people, who were all assembled at the foot of Mount Sinai, through his intermediary, Moses—their leader—some seven weeks after the exodus from Egypt (c. 1500 B.C.).

The Torah which God gave Moses was in two forms:
—the written Torah,
—the oral Torah.

According to Jewish tradition, God revealed the Torah in 70 languages so that it could be learnt by all the nations of the earth, but only the children of Israel fully embraced the "yoke of the kingdom of heaven," declaring: "We shall carry out [your precepts], then we shall understand."

 The written Torah
This is the Bible, or what for the Christians is the "Old Testament." The *Pentateuch* forms its center part and is a closely interwoven combination of:
—history (from the creation of the world to the death of Moses);
—a moral and legal code, encapsulated in the
Ten Commandments.

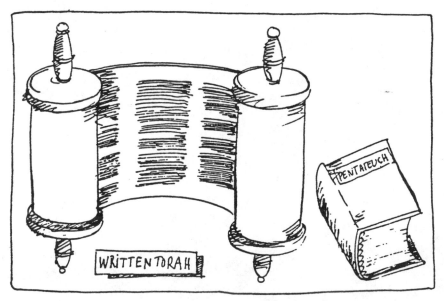

WRITTEN TORAH

PENTATEUCH

THE PENTATEUCH WAS DICTATED TO MOSES BY GOD HIMSELF. IT IS THEREFORE PARTICULARLY SACRED. AN ARMY OF SCRIBES IN EACH GENERATION HAS BEEN CHARGED WITH THE TASK OF TRANSCRIBING THE TEXT, AND EVERY SYNAGOGUE HAS AT LEAST ONE COPY.

Each Sabbath a passage from the scrolls of the Pentateuch is read in public.

The Torah is the "marriage contract" between God and Israel that defines the mutual obligations of the spouses.

The scrolls are particularly venerated and loved since they recall the history of the human race and of the Jewish people, and contain the divine word. One festival in particular celebrates "the Joy of the Torah." It is a time of rejoicing and **dancing with the Torah.**

55

But the written Torah cannot be considered to be a satisfactory guide, since the laws are set out in an obscure, sometimes even incomprehensible, manner. The precepts of the written Torah can only be applied in practical terms if clarified by commentaries. This is the role of the oral Torah, which has been handed down and taught from generation to generation since Moses.

If the written Torah is common to Jews, Christians and in part to Moslems, **the oral Torah is specific to Jews.** Judaism stresses the **practical application of the divine word in every sphere of life,** and the oral Torah is precisely what enables this to happen.

Examples:
1. Written Torah: "You shall not cook a kid in its mother's milk." The oral Torah instructs that this is a law which forbids Jews to eat meat and milk together.

2. Written Torah: On the Sabbath "You shall do no work." But what is "work?" The oral Torah enumerates 39 activities which are forbidden on the Sabbath (see chapter on Sabbath, p. 100).

■ **The oral Torah** = the *Mishnah*, the *Gemara*, the *Talmud*.

WHY IS IT CALLED THE ORAL TORAH?

BECAUSE IT IS FORBIDDEN TO WRITE DOWN ALL THESE INSTRUCTIONS! IT IS IMPORTANT NOT TO SET DOWN ORAL LAW, WHICH IS INTENDED TO DEAL WITH EVER-CHANGING CONCRETE PROBLEMS.

59

This is how the *Mishnah* first came into being. It succinctly expounds the precepts of Jewish law in methodical fashion and is subdivided into six "orders":

Agriculture—prayers . . .
Sabbath and festivals . . .
Family life . . .
Civil and criminal law . . .
Temple service . . .
Purity and impurity . . .

In fact the explanations and clarifications of the *Mishnah* themselves became the subject of innumerable rabbinic commentaries throughout many generations. These are collectively known as the *Gemara*.

These debates were collected together and written down in the two great spiritual centers of Judaism of that age: Babylon and Palestine.

Mishnah + Gemara = Talmud

The Babylonian Talmud (the most important) = 5th century.

The Jerusalem Talmud = 4th century.

Once the mammoth task of compiling the work was complete, the Talmud became the true spiritual homeland of the exiles.

Thus the Talmud became the source of Jewish law, or *Halachah* in Hebrew = to walk (the path of righteousness). But also . . .

. . . to walk = to evolve and not to stand still.
    The *Halachah* is intended to respond to new problems, which
may not have existed at the time the Talmud was written.

> ALL WORK IS FORBIDDEN ON THE SABBATH BUT IS SWITCHING ON THE ELECTRICITY 'WORK'?

> DO THE NEW METHODS OF CONTRACEPTION COMPLY WITH THE LAW?

> IN MODERN-DAY ISRAEL - CAN ECONOMIC LIFE CARRY ON DURING THE SABBATH?

> ETC.

Oral law is not only legislative in nature (*Halachah*), but also
has a narrative and moral element, the *Aggadah* (the sayings,
or "tales" of the Lord).

> ..THEN HE PREACHED THAT CHARITY CAN SAVE YOU FROM DEATH....

> ... THE JUST ARE GREATER THAN THE ANGELS OF THE LORD....

The oral Torah—the Midrash

The *Midrash* exists alongside the Talmud and is a collection of explanatory texts: *Midrash* = examine the text in depth (in order to learn).

An example taken from the *Midrash*:

WRITTEN TORAH: "GOD BROUGHT HIM (ABRAHAM) OUTSIDE AND SAID:' LOOK UP AND COUNT THE STARS...'"

"...BROUGHT HIM OUTSIDE" = HE BROUGHT HIM OUTSIDE THE WORLD.
"...AND SAID LOOK UP... AND COUNT THE STARS..." = LOOK DOWN AT THE STARS FROM UP ABOVE, FOR YOU ARE ABOVE THE STARS, WHICH ARE DETERMINED BY CAUSES!

IN THIS WAY, GOD SHOWED ABRAHAM THAT THE FATE OF THE JEWISH PEOPLE IS NOT IN THE HANDS OF HISTORY BUT DIRECTLY IN HIS HANDS.

The Kabbala
This is an esoteric commentary on the Torah, also handed down after Mount Sinai (Kabbalah = transmission). The best-known work of the Kabbala is the *Zohar* (13th century?).

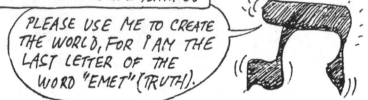

> TO CREATE THE WORLD, GOD WITHDREW, AND BY THIS ACTION OF "ZIMZUM" OR CONTRACTION CREATED A PLACE FOR IT.

> TWO THOUSAND YEARS BEFORE THE CREATION THE LETTERS OF THE ALPHABET APPEARED BEFORE THE CREATOR. THE LETTER 'TAV' ת – LAST LETTER OF THE ALPHABET-APPEARED FIRST, SAYING:

> PLEASE USE ME TO CREATE THE WORLD, FOR I AM THE LAST LETTER OF THE WORD "EMET" (TRUTH).

The problem of the "contradiction"
The traditional Jewish approach to the "contradictions" raised by the Torah text can hardly fail to bemuse the Western mind. In fact . . .

> FAR FROM INVALIDATING A TEXT, THE "CONTRADICTION" IS SIMPLY A CHALLENGE TO THE POWER OF INTERPRETATION...

> ..FOR EVERY WORD, EVERY LETTER OF THE TORAH IS SIGNIFICANT...

> ... AND THE TORAH-THE DIVINE WORD - CANNOT CON- -TAIN INTERNAL CONTRADICTIONS.

Example: "She (woman) shall be a helper against him" (man). Is she a helper? Is she against him? (Answer: see p. 90.)

The study of the Torah

According to tradition, studying the Torah—the divine word—is the ultimate Jewish activity.

"Study of the Torah is above the commandments." This is why the Jewish world quickly came to establish a highly sophisticated scholastic system, which the texts define in very precise terms.

"Any town without a school shall be excommunicated."
(Maimonides)

An extension of the elementary educational system is the *Yeshivah*, which is a Jewish school of the highest standard, where both young and old may continue their studies on a permanent basis.

But the obligation to study goes well beyond the scholastic institutions.

Torah study is compulsory for every Jew . . .

(maimonides)

The ideal suggested by the Talmud is to work just long enough to be able to subsist in order to spend the rest of the the day studying.

This obligation accounts for the *Yeshivot* springing up all over the world, though no one is exempted from daily study.

This appears to be the origin of the **Jewish love of culture** (particularly after the emancipation), and the Jewish peoples contribution to man's cultural heritage.

MY SON THE DOCTOR!

Jewish Ethics
Jewish Society

When God gave Moses the Ten Commandments ("ten words"), they were engraved on **two** stone tablets.

One gave the **vertical commandments**, i.e., those governing **man's relationship with God.**

The other gave the **horizontal commandments**, i.e., those governing **man's relationship with man.**

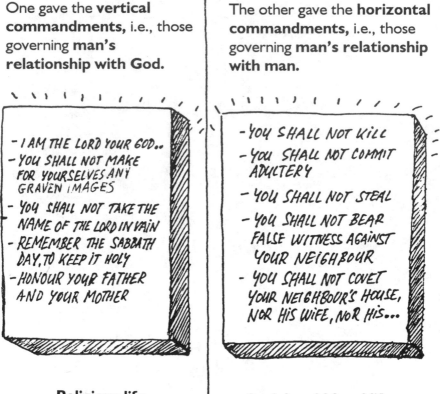

- I AM THE LORD YOUR GOD..
- YOU SHALL NOT MAKE FOR YOURSELVES ANY GRAVEN IMAGES
- YOU SHALL NOT TAKE THE NAME OF THE LORD IN VAIN
- REMEMBER THE SABBATH DAY, TO KEEP IT HOLY
- HONOUR YOUR FATHER AND YOUR MOTHER

- YOU SHALL NOT KILL
- YOU SHALL NOT COMMIT ADULTERY
- YOU SHALL NOT STEAL
- YOU SHALL NOT BEAR FALSE WITNESS AGAINST YOUR NEIGHBOUR
- YOU SHALL NOT COVET YOUR NEIGHBOUR'S HOUSE, NOR HIS WIFE, NOR HIS...

Religious life

Social and Moral life

The two tablets were given at the same time, and tradition tells us that . . .

The ten words were expressed as a single word.

This means that in Judaism the religious sphere encompasses all aspects of life: not just religious observance in the strictest sense, but also social and moral life, as indicated by the words:

"...follow the path of the Lord our God by practicing virtue and justice."

and . . .

"Love your neighbor as yourself"—one of the fundamental principles of the Torah.

and also . . .

Thus, social and community life are an integral part of Jewish tradition:

"Love your work"

In Judaism, work has intrinsic value. Work constitutes an obligation . . .

Even in the Garden of Eden, God obliged man to "cultivate and take care of" the garden.

. . .regardless of the results achieved.

God is the real source of any wealth.

(This is also why it is **forbidden to waste money,** or anything else.)

Then there is the dignity of work . . .

For this reason a legal system governing work has evolved since the biblical era.

Examples:

The rights of the slave = slavery, which was permissible in biblical times, was moderated by several obligations.

Generally speaking, Jewish tradition seems to base the preservation of human dignity on the following theory:

God is the true ruler. And "slavery in the service of God" signifies the attainment of true liberty. It is written that: "Whosoever accepts the yoke of the Torah (divine law) shall be liberated from the yoke of power."

Judaism and politics

Judaism retains a traditional mistrust of political power. Let us take you back 2600 years:

Jewish tradition favors a healthy respect for power, however . . .

OTHERWISE THE INHABITANTS OF THE TOWN WOULD TEAR EACH OTHER TO PIECES!

. . . and the ideals of the good citizen =

"THE LAW OF THE LAND (IN WHICH YOU LIVE) SHALL PREVAIL! "

GOD, BLESS THE LEADERS OF OUR LAND WITH PROSPERITY!

If the law of the land forces Jews to transgress the Torah:
Their duty is to prefer death to transgression, to defend themselves or to leave the country.

Tzedukah. The usual translation "charity" is too wide; this sort of charity costs money!

It actually means:

ZEDAKAH - ZEDAK = JUSTICE

God is the provider of all riches. According to Jewish tradition, if He is more generous to some than to others, it is in order to **give mankind the chance to redistribute the wealth.**

Thus, *Tzedukah* is not a favor which is granted, but a **duty** incumbent upon all, including the poor. The amount is not left up to the individual to decide, but is fixed at 10% of net income (or one-tenth of your produce).

 Gemilut Hassadim—acts of loving kindness.
Even better than *Tzedukah*.

1. Can be dispensed as much with words as with money . . .
2. . . . .not only to the poor, but also to the rich...

3. . . . .to the dead, as well as the living . . . = the dead should be accompanied to their final resting place.

Jewish law gives precise instructions regarding the nature of the welfare work to be carried out:
—visiting the sick
—staying with the dead until burial
—interest-free capital loans
—maintenance of students

In this way, communities were gradually able to establish an institutional infrastructure, which helped to ease the rigors of exile. Welfare funds, capital loans, finance for schools, etc.

The ideal is giving, not to maintain but to grant **independence.**
(Hebrew: welfare = gomel = to wear.)

QUESTION?

CAN'T YOU SEE THERE ONE OF THE ORIGINS OF THE GROWTH OF TRADE-UNIONISM AMONG THE JEWISH PROLETARIAT OF EUROPE? ...AND, MORE GENERALLY, THE POLITICI--ZATION AND MASS PARTICIPATION IN SOCIALIST MOVEMENTS?

...AS WELL AS THE COOPERATIVE MOVEMENT IN ISRAEL?

 Love your neighbor
       All these prescriptions are closely linked to the Torah principle:

> 'Love your neighbour as yourself.'

Judaism is anxious to translate this ideal into action, for example:

. . . according to tradition, it is only by **serving our neighbor** that we are able to strengthen our love for him or her. Example: the strong bond between parent and child is to large extent the result of the effort put into the relationship:

Humility

Humility before God, but also before man:
—to abstain rigorously from scandal-mongering
—to practice hospitality
—not to hate one's neighbor in one's heart.

 Striving for peace
among nations as well as among individuals:

 The stranger

 Respect for life

To Judaism, human life is sacred: after all, man was created in the image of God.

Where there is the slightest possibility of mortal danger, breaking a commandment is virtually compulsory, if it will save life (see p. 109).

Marriage and family life

One of the most respected figures of the Catholic ethic is the celibate, the priest or nun practicing complete sexual abstinence. Conversely, the Jewish ideal is marriage and procreation, both of which are obligatory for a man. Marriage is not considered a concession to the weakness of the flesh, but the path to personal fulfillment for both husband and wife.

We read in the Bible that the Jews do not consider the cardinal sin to be "the sin of the flesh."

Family life—meaning the couple, **independently of the duty to procreate**—is central to Jewish life, even more so than the Synagogue. "The home is a Temple and the family table the altar" (Talmud). It is here that the Jew must practice love of his neighbor—**his neighbor being his or her spouse.**

The Couple

Basic equality of men and women: the first human being was both male and female. The Bible tells us: "Male and female He created them."

Complementary nature of men and women: to create Woman, God "took one of his ribs," which the commentary misreads as "one of his sides" . . .

IT IS NOT GOOD FOR ADAM TO BE ALONE ... WITH HIS POWER COMPLEX, HE MIGHT JUST THINK HE IS ME.....!

In other words, to create Woman, God separated the feminine from the masculine part.

85

Different natures, different roles:
Man's nature is essentially **spiritual:**
His functions are:
—worship
—study of the Torah
—the pursuit of external
activities = work, public
life, etc.

Whereas **woman . . .**

. . . is linked to the material world.

...THE ROLE IN NO WAY IMPLIES INFERIORITY. NOR WILL THE SAGE SUGGEST THAT A MAN SHOULD LOVE HIS WIFE LESS, FOR YOU MUST "LOVE YOUR WIFE LIKE YOUR OWN BODY!" (RABBI LOEW (YEHUDI BEL BETSALEL 16th CENT, PRAGUE) WROTE IN AN ERA WHEN SOME QUESTIONED WHETHER WOMEN HAD SOULS...)

In no way is the material world held in contempt by Jewish tradition: "and God saw that it was good." Human beings have been set the task of improving the creation by their actions.

SEEN IN THIS LIGHT, THE ROLE OF WOMAN IS FUNDAMENTAL: TO TRANS--LATE JUDAISM INTO FAMILY LIFE. "THE HOME IS A TEMPLE AND THE TABLE, THE ALTAR."

MORE PRECISELY, WOMEN HAVE THE FOLLOWING (HEAVY) RESPONSIBILITIES:

FIRST, TO EDUCATE THE CHILDREN AND TRANSMIT JEWISH VALUES. DEFINITION OF A JEW ACCORDING TO JEWISH LAW: ONE BORN OF A JEWISH MOTHER (SEE P. 97).

STRICT OBSERVANCE OF THE DIETARY LAWS (SEE P. 137).

KEEPING FESTIVALS AND PREPARING TRADITIONAL DISHES (SEE P. 114 FOR THEIR SYMBOLIC IMPORTANCE).

WOMEN MAY WORK OUTSIDE THE HOME BUT NOT TO THE DETRIMENT OF FAMILY LIFE.

89

On the other hand, woman is called:
"a helper against him [man]."
In other words, she supports him in his fight against his baser nature.

Alternatively:
"a helper against" . . .
Is he deserving? His wife will be **a helper.**
Is he undeserving? His wife will be **against him.**

The only legal framework for the male/female relationship is marriage.

In the biblical era polygamy was tolerated, although monogamy was still preferred as the ideal. In the West, polygamy has been banned since the 10th century. The ideal to aim for in marriage is total union: **"and you shall be one flesh."**

The divine presence itself presides over a united home.

IN OTHER WORDS, AS USUAL, A WIFE MUST SACRIFICE HERSELF FOR HER HUSBAND?

YES, BUT THE HUSBAND SHOULD DO THE SAME. IT SAYS...

"HONOUR YOUR WIFE MORE THAN YOUR OWN BODY!"

AND LOVE?

ACCORDING TO THE KABBALA, THE SOUL SPLITS IN TWO BEFORE IT DESCENDS TO EARTH, AND EACH HALF SETTLES IN A BODY OF A DIFFERENT SEX....

THIS ALL SEEMS VERY FAR REMOVED FROM THE ROMANTIC IDEAL OF AN ALL-CONSUMING PASSION. IN HEBREW, LOVE = YODEA = TO KNOW. THE RELATION--SHIP SHOULD NOT BE BASED ON MERE FLEETING PHYSICAL ATTRACTION.

THE TRICK IS TO FIND THE RIGHT HALF!

DO YOU BELIEVE THAT?

Thus, far from being indifferent, the successful couple should find that love grows the more they get to know each other.

Sex

Sexual activity occupies an accepted place in the life of the couple, not only for the purposes of procreation, but also to strengthen the bond with mutual pleasure.

p.s. The Kabbala says that it is good to lie with your wife on the Sabbath, for in this way husband and wife share in the unity of the cosmos.

Divorce:

The role of the couple is an essential one, yet divorce **is perfectly legitimate,** for the sake of a realistic approach. But—unlike contemporary society—Judaism refuses to play down the seriousness of a divorce.

Even the stones of the temple altar lament a separation. . . .

In biblical times divorce was by repudiation . . . the husband simply repudiated his wife . . .

THOSE WERE THE DAYS!

. . . but in the 10th century a system close to divorce by common consent was introduced. Also, the compulsory drawing up of a **marriage contract,** or *ketubbah*, lays down the terms of separation:

IF YOU WISH TO REPUDIATE ME...

..YOU MUST:
1. OBTAIN MY CONSENT...

2. RETURN MY DOWRY A CONSIDERABLE SUM WHICH IS SPECIFIED IN THE MARRIAGE CONTRACT...

..WHICH YOU WERE FOOLISH ENOUGH TO SIGN!

Family life
Jews have an obligation to have a family.

Only a chain of successive generations can ensure that the divine purpose is accomplished—the preparation of humanity for the revelation of God.

Parents and children have mutual obligations.

Obligation of the parents:
To provide for the physical well-being of the child, but also to **transmit Jewish values.**

Moreover, of the two parents, in terms of transmitting Judaism, it is the **mother who is given the role of principal educator,** according to the texts.

Remember that Jewish law defines the Jew as "one born of a Jewish mother."

It is the mother who remains responsible for organizing the Jewish home and for creating a special atmosphere which will stay with the child for the rest of its life.

I REMEMBER SITTING AT THE SABBATH TABLE WITH THE THREE LIGHTED CANDLES, THE FESTIVE TABLE, WHICH WAS ALREADY A SMALL PART OF THE MESSIAH'S KINGDOM, WITH MY MOTHER. (ALBERT COHEN, THE BOOK OF MY MOTHER)

SZLAK MANN

From Jewish society the character of the **Jewish mother** has emerged, a favorite of New York Jewish literature, a mother smothering her son with an excessive and emasculating love.

Obligations of the child:

"Honor your father and your mother." Jewish law is very strict on this point, considering the parents as "representatives" of God with regard to the child. The obligations of the child towards his parents are:

—to keep them (if they are poor)
—to serve them at table
—not to answer back rudely, etc.

How far should these obligations be taken?

The Talmud quotes a non-Jew as an example: "[This man] was presiding over a municipal council. Once, his mother hit him about the head before the entire assembly. The shoe she was hitting him with slipped out of her hand. He picked it up and gave it to her. . . ."

To honor your father and mother is good preparation for "loving your neighbor" as demanded by Jewish tradition.

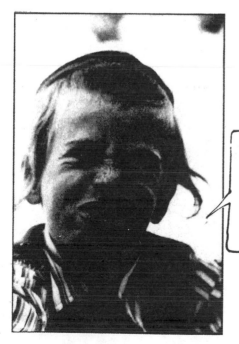

HOWEVER, THE CHILD MUST DISOBEY IF THE PARENTS TELL HIM TO TRANSGRESS THE TORAH! (BUT EVEN THEN, THE CHILD MUST DO SO WITHOUT RUDENESS....)

The Sabbath

This is the most important institution in Judaism. No work may be carried out on the Sabbath from sunset on Friday evening to sunset on Saturday evening.

"In six days, God created heaven and earth and on the seventh day, He rested."

WHO ME? THE ALL POWERFUL! WHO SAYS I NEED A REST?!

WELL... THAT IS.. BY "REST" THE BIBLE MEANS THAT ALL MATERIALLY CREATIVE WORK SHOULD CEASE (EARTH, SEA, STARS, ETC.) BUT NOT THAT ALL ACTIVITY SHOULD STOP: ACTUALLY, GOD CREATED THE SOUL, WHICH EVERY HUMAN BEING HAS, ON THE SEVENTH DAY!

PRECISELY! THE MATERIAL WORLD IS NOT, IN ITSELF, AN END, BUT PROVIDES SUPPORT FOR THE SPIRITUAL LIFE....

... AND THE SOUL IS THE PINNACLE OF CREATION, JUST AS THE SEVENTH DAY, THE SABBATH, IS THE HIGH POINT OF THE WEEK.

THE SABBATH SHOULD THUS BE DEVOTED TO SPIRITUAL LIFE.

But the Sabbath also has a social significance: proclaiming the dignity of all mankind.

". . . and you shall remember that you were **slaves** in the land of Egypt and that **the Lord your God has commanded you to keep the Sabbath!**"

The granting of a weekly day of rest for all men without exception amounts to the slave achieving the status of a free man—at least for one day of the week!

How does the Jew observe the Sabbath?

—he or she observes a series of prohibitions.

—he or she devotes himself to the "joy of the Sabbath" by carrying out certain activities.

  Sabbath dos and don'ts
"You shall do no work on the Sabbath."

The term "work" is **not related to the amount of physical effort expended:**

OR HANDLING MONEY...

Generally speaking, how do you define "work"?
It covers **any activity which may be carried out in connection with production or trade, however indirect.**

Examples:

—**carrying** an object away from or to the home: this could lead to bartering.
—**switching on power,** even for domestic purposes: radio, television, lighting . . .
—**using muscle power,** even without intending to work: digging a hole in the ground (= manual labor), watering the ground (= irrigation) . . .
—**money,** all handling is forbidden, including the **verbal** conclusion of a business deal.

IT IS NO HARDSHIP FOR THE PIOUS JEW TO OBSERVE THE SABBATH RESTRICTIONS!

What is the point of this break in normal life?

 Recognition of the absolute sovereignty of God over the universe:

God is not only the Creator, but also the **Animator** of the universe.

By voluntary cessation of all financial and physical activity, **even if this means financial loss,** the Jew proclaims that human effort is rewarded only **if this is the will of God.**

You will regard all your work as completed by the sixth day, and you will put your trust in Him. . . .

But the sovereignty of man over the earth must also be proclaimed.

By voluntary interrupting his commercial activities, the Jew consciously refuses to become the "slave of progress."

The Sabbath is thus an attempt to ensure that everyone retains a modicum of dignity, regardless of circumstances, and can enjoy a weekly day of rest, even those at the bottom of the ladder.

The prohibitions of the Sabbath should be carried out to the letter.

But the Sabbath should not be a day of mortification or asceticism. On the contrary:
"It is forbidden to fast on Sabbath.
It is a day of light for all Israel
And you shall call the Sabbath a day of delight."

How to enjoy the Sabbath in comfort, despite Sabbath interdictions:

Some real problems:

As the sayings go:

> "The Sabbath was given to Israel and not Israel to the Sabbath".—and "Observe my precepts and **live!**"

But the joy of the Sabbath is contained in the combination of ceremonies and activities, which gives the Sabbath its special atmosphere.

1. As for most of the Jewish festivals, the family home must be cleaned and prepared to welcome the Sabbath as an honored guest: the Sabbath is the **"bride of Israel."**

2. At dusk the mistress of the house lights two candles, which are symbolic of the original light hidden by God when Adam and Eve sinned.

THE REKINDLING OF THE
"ORIGINAL LIGHT" IS
A RESPONSIBILITY
GIVEN TO THE WOMAN,
QUEEN OF THE HOME.

3. The evening is consecrated by a festive meal attended by the whole family. The meal starts with . . .

After the meal the family usually sings and talks long into the night.

4. Saturday is spent praying, studying, and eating another meal
with the family.
Sabbath is a time for family reunion, when each family member
can rest from the stresses and strains of daily life . . .

It is also another opportunity for a Jew to pursue the study of the
Torah, either at a synagogue or at home.
In conclusion, no Sabbath meal is complete without guests,
whether these are travelers, or poor or deprived people invited in.

When Sabbath begins, the Jew radiates a special glow:
God gives him an "extra Sabbath soul".

The Sabbath is a foretaste of the messianic age.

The Jewish Calendar

The Jewish calendar is calculated from the time of creation:

e.g., 1986 = the year 5746, i.e., 5746 years since the creation.
The Jewish calendar is both solar and lunar.
—Solar: the year has 365 days.
—Lunar: the cycle of months corresponds to the cycle of lunar rotations.
There are thus 12 months of 29 or 30 days and an additional month in certain years to bring the calendar into line with the solar year.
Jewish tradition perceives a number of affinities between the moon and Israel.

SUN = REPRESENTATION OF MATERIAL POWER. THE PREROGATIVE OF NATIONS.

MOON = WEAK RAY OF LIGHT IN THE KINGDOM OF THE NIGHT = ISRAEL HUMILIATED AMONG NATIONS IN THE LONG NIGHT OF EXILE. SUBTLE INFLUENCE OF THE MOON = GRADUAL PENETRATION OF JEWISH IDEOLOGY.

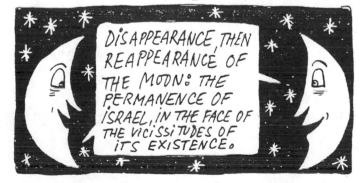

DISAPPEARANCE, THEN REAPPEARANCE OF THE MOON: THE PERMANENCE OF ISRAEL, IN THE FACE OF THE VICISSITUDES OF ITS EXISTENCE.

The Jewish year is interspersed with a number of festivals.

These festivals involve a series of prohibitions and specific commands:
—a special synagogue service
—at the family table, in some cases, various dishes served are composed of different foods symbolizing the divine word.

—Finally, almost every festival has a triple significance:
1) it denotes a natural or agricultural event.
2) it commemorates a historical event.
3) it has a metaphysical meaning.

The New Year—*Rosh Hashanah* (around September). This is the "birthday of the world." On this day, God opens the **"Book of Life"** and records individual's deeds throughout the year.

"... AND I SHALL PASS BEFORE GOD FOR JUDGEMENT, AS THE SHEEP PASS BEFORE THE WATCHFUL EYE OF THE SHEPHERD."

In the service, the *shofar*—**a ram's horn without blemish**— is sounded.

WHY THE SHOFAR?

Well, one day God said to Abraham:

This is why the ram's horn speaks directly to God...

> GOD! HAVE MERCY! REMEMBER ABRAHAM, READY TO MAKE THE SACRIFICE!

...and also to the Jews...

> JEWS! REMEMBER THE EXAMPLE OF YOU FOREFATHER ABRAHAM READY TO MAKE THE SACRIFICE!

to remind them to examine their consciences.

As with most Jewish festivals certain traditional foods have evolved. At the family meal, an apple is dipped in **honey**, for a "sweet" year.

> HAPPY NEW YEAR!

> HAPPY NEW YEAR!

> HAPPY NEW YEAR!

> A YEAR OF PEACE! FOR ISRAEL AND ALL HUMANITY!

> A YEAR OF PROSPERITY

Rosh Hashanah is followed by "ten days of penitence" which culminate on the tenth day, the Day of Atonement.

The Day of Atonement: *Yom Kippur* (around September).

"ON ROSH HASHANAH I OPENED THE BOOK OF LIFE AND AT THE END OF YOM KIPPUR I SHALL CLOSE IT AGAIN; AND YOUR FATE WILL BE SEALED FOR THE COMING YEAR."

FASTING IS COMPULSORY FOR ALL ADULTS (NO EATING OR DRINKING FOR 25 HOURS).

THE DAY IS SPENT AT THE SYNAGOGUE IN PRAYER AND SUPPLICATION...

...ASKING FOR GOD'S FORGIVENESS.

119

Most members of the Jewish community, even those who are not very orthodox, observe *Yom Kippur*—at least partially—and go to the synagogue, even if they never go again during the rest of the year.

This is in fact **the only festival which has no historical base whatsoever:** it has a purely religious meaning. Israel, faithful bride of God?

The Feast of the Tabernacles: *Succot* (around October)

For eight days Jews are obliged to eat and sleep—weather permitting—in a temporary structure in the open air called a "booth," which has a roof made of leaves.

Rejoicing the Law: *Simchath Torah.*
The day of *Simchath Torah* marks the conclusion of the reading cycle of the Torah, and its **immediate recommencement** from the beginning. **This signifies the infinite nature of spiritual progression:** as with the Torah reading, it must constantly begin anew.

The Torah scrolls are read aloud in the synagogue every Sabbath—the Torah is divided into 52 parts, one for each week, from Genesis to the death of Moses.

On *Simchath Torah* the Jew dances with the Torah, as a man
dances with his wife, to demonstrate his love.

The Festival of Light: *Hanukkah* (around December).
This commemorates the following miracle:
In the 2nd century B.C., the Jews succeeded in driving the Greco-Syrians from the land of Israel. When it came to kindling the Temple lights, they discovered a cruse of oil containing only enough oil to last for one day, but which sufficed for **eight days.**
(Eight days = the time required to obtain more oil.)

HANUKKAH DOES NOT THEREFORE COMMEMORATE A MILITARY VICTORY, BUT THE MIRACLE OF THE LIGHT: — A VICTORY OF THE SPIRITUAL OVER THE MATERIAL — A VICTORY OF THE WEAK OVER THE STRONG!

THE CHILDREN OF ISRAEL REFUSED TO ABANDON THEIR VALUES, DESPITE VARIOUS ATTEMPTS AT SEDUCING THEM AWAY AND THEN THE VIOLENCE EXERCISED BY THE GREEKS.

The Festival of Lots: *Purim* (around March)

The Vizier of the Persian king, Ahasuerus (5th century B.C.), issued a proclamation that all Jews in the empire should be put to death. But a young Jewess, **Esther**, boldly interceded with the king, who eventually reversed the infamous decree. *Purim* commemorates this event.

PURIM IS A JOYFUL FESTIVAL...

...AND AS IT COMMEMORATES A PHYSICAL THREAT OF GENOCIDE IT IS PRECISELY THE MATERIAL ASPECT, WHICH IS IMPORTANT: FESTIVE MEAL PLENTY TO DRINK, GIFTS, ETC...

On *Purim* the reading is taken from a scroll called the "Book of Esther" (*Megillat Esther*), which relates the story.

125

Passover: *Pesach* (around April)

This commemorates the **liberation of the Jews** from slavery in Egypt.

—**The Spring festival:** Israel bursting forth from Egypt, like buds bursting into bloom. The central focus of the festival is the ritual meal called the *seder*, during which it is incumbent upon the father, or head of the household, to read the *hagadah*, which relates the story of the Exodus from Egypt.

—It is forbidden to eat any *h'ametz*, or cereal products, which could ferment = bread or dough.

—only *matsoh*—**unleavened bread** (without yeast) can be eaten. (Passover = feast of unleavened bread.)

The centerpiece of the *seder* table is the ritual dish, with its **symbolic foods.**

BITTER HERBS, A REMINDER OF THE BITTERNESS OF SLAVERY.

FIGS AND GROUND ALMONDS TO REMIND US OF THE MORTAR USED IN BUILDING WORK

 The Feast of Weeks (Pentecost): *Shevuot* (around May)

Seven weeks after the Exodus from Egypt the Jews were given the Torah on Mount Sinai. This event is commemorated by *Shevout*. It coincides with the beginning of the summer grain and fruit harvest in ancient Palestine.

THE TORAH DOES NOT GIVE A PRECISE DATE FOR SHAVUOT: THE TORAH IS BEYOND TIME. THE LOCATION OF MOUNT SINAI IS NOT GIVEN EXACTLY: THE TORAH IS BEYOND SPACE.

Fast of the 9th of Av (around August)

Unlike the fast of *Yom Kippur*, the fast (25 hours) of the 9th of Av is a sign of mourning, in memory of the destruction of the **two** Temples of Jerusalem. A series of somber events occurred on the 9th of Av:

—fall of the last Jewish stronghold to the Romans (135)

—expulsion of the Jews from Spain (1492)

—outbreak of the First World War.

There is a story...

Ritual

 The practice of Judaism is not just spiritual, and tradition imposes the use of certain sacred objects.

These are in no way talismen, however—they have no value, other than as repositories for the divine word, as constant reminders of our obligations.

The prayer shawl and its fringes (*talit* and *tsitsit*). At morning prayers the Jew wraps himself in his prayer shawl, which is a rectangular piece of cloth with twisted strands at each of the four corners(*tsitsit*).

SOME JEWS CONTINUE TO WEAR SMALL TALITS UNDER THEIR OUTER CLOTHING THROUGHOUT THE DAY.

THE TSITSIT ARE MADE UP OF 39 STRANDS, BECAUSE 39 = NUMERIC VALUE OF THE LETTERS MAKING UP "GOD IS ONE" IN HEBREW.

WHEN YOU SEE THEM (THE TSITSIT) YOU WILL REMEMBER THE COMMANDMENTS!

HEBREW LETTERS ARE ALSO NUMERALS, SO ANY WORD HAS A NUMERICAL VALUE. GEMATRIA IS A MYSTICAL SYSTEM IN WHICH WORDS ARE SUBSTITUTED ON THE BASIS OF THEIR NUMERICAL VALUE TO REVEAL NEW MEANINGS.

The Phylacteries (*tefilin*)

These are two boxes of leather, each containing parchment, and each attached to a leather thong.

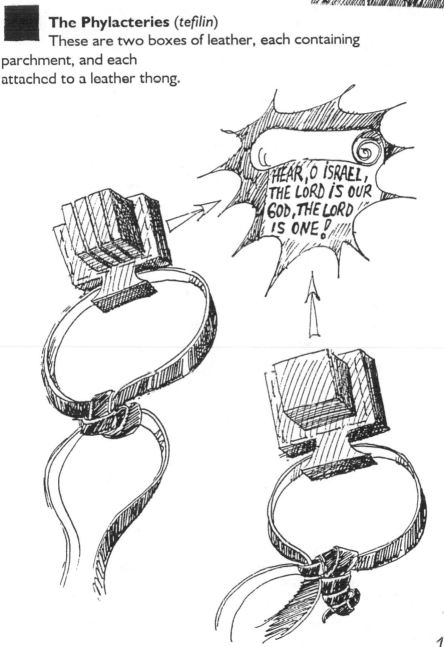

The *tefilin* are the crowning glory of the Jew. Just as the Jew must "ingest" the word of the Lord during festivals, he must also **wrap himself** in the divine word.

THEN THE OTHER BOX IS PLACED ON THE FOREHEAD: SYMBOLIC OF SERVING GOD WITH THE INTELECT.

④

①
FIRST, ONE BOX IS BOUND TO THE ARM, SYMBOLIC OF SERVING GOD WITH ONE'S BODY.

THE TONG IS WRAPPED SEVEN TIMES ⊙

②

THE TONG SHOULD THEN BE WRAPPED AROUND THE FINGER WHICH SYMBOLIZES THAT ISRAEL IS THE "BRIDE" OF THE LORD.

③

THERE IS NO INTERRUPTION BETWEEN THE PUTTING ON OF THE TEFILIN OF THE ARM AND OF THE HEAD, JUST AS THERE IS NO GAP BETWEEN THOUGHT AND ACTION.

The Mezuzah

The Jew must also adorn his home with the word of the Lord: this is why a *mezuzah*, or small box containing a parchment text, is fixed to the door lintel of Jewish homes.

HEAR, O ISRAEL, THE LORD IS OUR GOD, THE LORD IS ONE!

The head gear:

JEWISH MALES WEAR A "KIPAH" OR SKULL CAP, AS A SIGN OF RESPECT BEFORE GOD.

All these objects, symbolizing the divine word, enable it to be spread in the material world, which is Israel's mission.

Prayer

Initially left to the discretion of the individual, communal prayer was codified and rendered compulsory after the destruction of the Temple.

In essence it has hardly changed in 2,000 years, though it has become enriched through the centuries.

The service is written down in prayer books, which are very similar all over the world, with some minor variations.

The prayers comprise:

—**Supplications,** almost always collective...

—Talmudic teachings

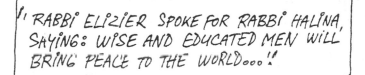

> "RABBI ELIZIER SPOKE FOR RABBI HALINA, SAYING: WISE AND EDUCATED MEN WILL BRING PEACE TO THE WORLD..."

—Historical events

> "AT THE TIME OF THE HIGH PRIEST MATITIAHOU,... THE TYRANICAL RULE OF GREECE WAS DIRECTED AGAINST YOUR PEOPLE, ISRAEL..."

—Praise

> "HOW GREAT ARE YOUR DEEDS, O LORD! THE EARTH IS FILLED WITH THE FRUITS OF YOUR LABOUR!"

Three important daily prayers:
—Morning prayers, where the texts place emphasis on the **clarity of vision** of the Almighty (approximately three-quarters of an hour).
—Afternoon prayers, which demand an interruption from the daily routine (approximately half an hour).
—Evening prayers, which proclaim faith and confidence in God at the onset of the shadowy uncertainty of the night.

Communal prayer (with a minimum of ten men) is better than individual prayer.

The Benedictions

Before any action of any significance is taken (eating, drinking, travel, getting up, carrying out a commandment, etc.) the faithful must make a corresponding pronouncement concerning the event.

For the Jew,
there is
no non-religious
act.

THIEF!

WHOSOEVER TAKES A PRODUCT OF MY CREATION WITHOUT PRONOUNCING THE BENEDICTION SHALL BE CALLED A THIEF!

'BLESSED ARE YOU, LORD OUR GOD... WHO BRINGS FORTH FOOD OUT OF THE EARTH!'

 # The Dietary Laws

Kashrut in Hebrew

Kosher food means food which **conforms** to the laws and is therefore fit for consumption. According to Jewish tradition, *Kashrut* is part of that reasoning which is beyond human comprehension: The Jew must simply have faith and accept. In line with most traditional schools of thought, Judaism affirms the existence of a link between what you eat and what you are.

Just as the Torah imposes restrictions on the sexual instinct, the self-preservation instinct (food) is also strictly regulated.

What are the laws of *Kashrut*?

Judaism endorses the consumption of meat.

Nevertheless, the *Midrash* says . . .

IF YOU DO NOT RESPECT MY COMMANDMENTS, THAT IS, YOUR SPECIAL ROLE AS HUMAN BEINGS, YOU SHALL BE LOWER THAN THE ANIMALS!

But not all meats are permitted.
Among mammals, only the following are kosher:
—quadrupeds   e.g., beef, lamb, etc.
—ruminants   All these animals are herbivores.
—cloven-hoofed animals

Those animals having only one or other or none of the above characteristics are forbidden.

Among birds:
Chicken, geese, ducks, etc. are permitted.
Birds of prey are forbidden.

FORBIDDEN

Among fish and aquatic animals:

ONLY FISH WITH FINS

...AND SCALES ARE PERMITTED.

FORBIDDEN:
EELS
RAYS
CRUSTACEANS
ETS.
AND SEAFOOD

Reptiles, mollusks:

FORBIDDEN

■ **Ritual slaughter of quadrupeds and poultry** (*shehita*):
Only certain individuals (*shotim*) are qualified to perform the ritual slaughter in all its meticulous detail.

The animal must be drained of blood, since, according to tradition, **Jews are forbidden to eat blood.**

■ **Prohibition against mixing dairy and meat.**
The separation principle, essential in Jewish practice (good, evil, clean, unclean . . .) is here as well.

The oral tradition forbids the mixing of dairy and meat.

"And you will not cook the kid with the milk of his mother. . . ."

FORBIDDEN

CHEESE
BACON-
BURGER, etc.

According to orthodox law, there must be a six hour interval between eating meat and dairy products.

Moreover, the kitchen must reflect this separation with two sets of pots or dishes.

In general, the Jewish dietary tradition is meant to create a feeling of internal peace.

use one set of dishes for dairy products...

... and another set for meats.

ISRAEL'S DESTINY

The chosen people.
"You have chosen us among all nations."
But this selection does not imply any superiority.

What is the meaning of this selection?
It achieves a spiritual mission.
—To make a dwelling for God in this world,
—To carry and pass down the divine message until the coming of the messianic age (see p. 161).

143

How is the mission to be accomplished?

By preserving (transmitting) and observing the Torah, the divine word.

Does this mean special privileges?
Quite the reverse!

IT IS YOU ALONE WHOM I HAVE DISTINGUISHED AMONG THE FAMILIES OF THE EARTH, AND THIS IS WHY YOU SHALL ACCOUNT FOR ALL YOUR FAULTS!

According to Jewish tradition, the "chosen" people were chosen to suffer, but also chosen out of love: Israel is called the "bride of God."

YOU HAVE MADE US ENDURE A THOUSAND HARDSHIPS, CAST OUT EVERYWHERE, CONDEMNED TO EXILE, BUT YOU WILL NEVER MAKE US GIVE IN: WE WILL ALWAYS HAVE FAITH IN YOU.

145

■ **The mission of the Jewish people is aimed at all humanity.**

In ancient Rome and under the Christians, Jewish proselytizing was extremely efficient . . .

. . . but this ceased with the restrictive measures.

It is also more in the spirit of Judaism to **act according to one's principles than to proclaim them.**

 Conversion to Judaism is however, possible:

"WHOEVER WISHES TO DO SO, MAY ENTER (INTO ALLIANCE WITH ISRAEL) AND SHALL BENEFIT FROM ITS BLESSINGS!

BUT THOSE WHO DO NOT WISH TO ENTER MAY ALSO OBEY THE TORAH BY OBSERVING THE COMMANDMENTS (SEVEN OF THEM) GIVEN BY GOD TO ALL NATIONS:

BE FAIR.

DO NOT BLASPHEME.

DO NOT KILL.

DO NOT STEAL.

DO NOT BEAR FALSE WITNESS.

DO NOT PRACTICE IDOLATRY.

DO NOT BEHAVE IN A BESTIAL FASHION.

But why exactly did God choose the Jewish people?

The commentary adds:
"This does not mean that you will be more numerous . . .,"
which is to say "you shall look on yourselves as small . . .," unlike
Nebuchadnezzar, who said: "I wish to resemble the Majesty of
the Almighty."

■ This process of selection was finalized by the ever-lasting covenant concluded between God and the Jewish people.

The symbol of this covenant is **circumcision**.

The elements of the covenant are:

—**The gift of the Torah** (see p. 52), the marriage contract between God and Israel.

—**the gift of the land of Israel.**

■ **Circumcision, symbol of the covenant** (*bris mila*— **covenant of circumcision**).

This is the removal of the foreskin, which must be carried out on the eighth day after the infant is born, providing the baby is well enough. It is a joyous family occasion.

The overwhelming majority of Jews, including nonpracticing Jews, continue to observe this commandment rigorously.

Through circumcision, the Jew places the divine seal on his most powerful instinct. He channels that instinct toward constructive behavior.

IT IS OBVIOUSLY NOT A QUESTION OF SUPPRESSING THE SEXUAL IMPULSE, WHICH IS NOT IN ITSELF AN EVIL...

...BUT RATHER CONTROLLING IT BY DISCIPLINE.

And, according to tradition, circumcision enables the Jewish male to do this.

THEREFORE, JUST AS A JEWISH MAN MUST DON THE EXTERNAL SYMBOLS OF THE COVENANT (TEFILINE, ETC.), HE MUST ALSO DON — ON HIS OWN FLESH, (CIRCUMCISION) — SUCH A SYMBOL.

The gift of the land of Israel

"For all the land which you see, to you will I give it and to your seed forever." This was the promise given to Abraham, which therefore pre-dates the existence of the Jews **as a people.**

In fact, the bond between the Jewish people and the land of Israel transcends any "territorial attachments." **It is a metaphysical bond.**

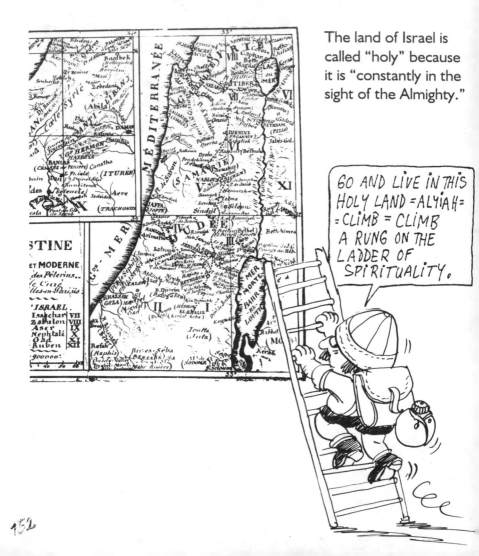

The land of Israel is called "holy" because it is "constantly in the sight of the Almighty."

GO AND LIVE IN THIS HOLY LAND =ALYIAH= = CLIMB = CLIMB A RUNG ON THE LADDER OF SPIRITUALITY.

God gave this Holy Land to the Jews forever. **But this possession is conditional!**

"IF YOU LIVE ACCORDING TO MY LAWS, YOU SHALL HAVE AN ABUNDANCE OF BREAD TO EAT AND YOU SHALL LIVE IN PEACE IN YOUR LAND. BUT...

BEWARE THAT THE LAND MAY NOT VOMIT YOU OUT..."

IN THIS WAY, JEWISH TRADITION ATTRIBUTES THE EXILES NOT TO MILITARY WEAKNESS IN THE FACE OF INVASIONS, BUT TO AN ABANDONMENT OF THE VALUES OF THE TORAH.

"IT IS FOR OUR SINS THAT WE WERE EXILED TO A DISTANT LAND!"

According to the commentators, the first Temple was destroyed because of —among other causes—non-observance of the laws concerning "Sabbath of rest for the Holy Land" and the "Jubilee."

The Law of Sabbath of rest for the land (valid only for the Holy Land)

The Law of Jubilee

This idea of a link between

moral conduct and **national sovereignty**

can be translated into modern terms as the link between

ethics and **politics.**

According to Jewish tradition, separation is not fatal.
Question: Is this where one finds the root of the democratic
structure in modern Israel?

In any event, even if effective possession of the land is conditional, **the link between the Jewish people and their land is, itself, eternal, and has never been diminished throughout the course of history.**

THERE HAS ALWAYS BEEN A JEWISH PRESENCE IN PALESTINE THROUGH THE AGES.

SHABETAI Z'VI (P.31) REVIVED THE SPIRIT OF THE JEWISH MASSES BY PROCLAI-MING THE RETURN TO THE HOLY LAND.

IN OUR TIMES, THE STATE OF ISRAEL (1948) IS WHAT BINDS JEWS ALL OVER THE WORLD TOGETHER.

THEODOR HERZL (1860-1904), FOUNDER OF POLITICAL ZIONISM

SZLAK MANN

For it is the symbolic meaning of **"Jerusalem of earth"** which is the focal point:

"Not until we have built Jerusalem on earth . . . will we achieve Jerusalem on high."

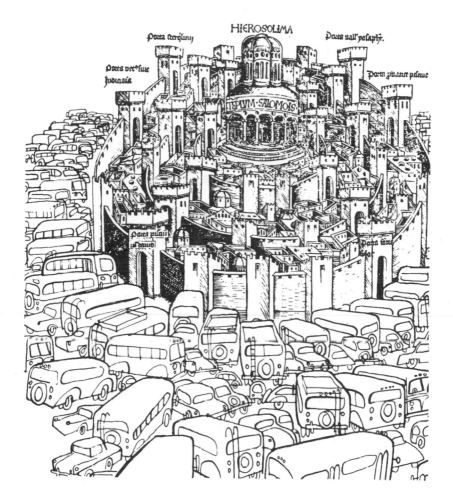

Drawing by Shmuel Katz.

In fact, the commentary states that the trials imposed on Israel, the "bride of God," are disproportionate to her infidelities.

And in Jewish tradition . . .

THE TARGETS OF THE ENEMIES OF ISRAEL ARE **GOD** HIMSELF AND HIS LAWS...

. . . this is where the root of anti-Semitism lies.

... ie. THE SYSTEM OF VALUES ENTRUSTED TO THE JEWISH PEOPLE.

SUCCESSIVE CONQUERORS WERE SIMPLY THE INSTRUMENTS OF GOD. THIS IS NOT TO SAY THAT THEY WERE INNOCENT — QUITE THE REVERSE...

SINCE THEY WERE LIKE ALL MEN GIVEN FREE WILL, THEY WERE RESPONSIBLE FOR THEIR ACTIONS AND THEREFORE IN TURN PUNISHED BY GOD.

Just as God cannot be destroyed, so Israel is indestructible. In this way, all the nations of the earth shall acknowledge the intervention of the Omnipotent in the destiny of Israel.

God may allow some of his people to perish, but even again from the ashes the people will arise.

Yet the genocide of 1939-45 does present contemporary Jewish thinkers with a **difficult question:**

"BLESSED BE THE LORD OUR GOD!"

BUT WHY SHOULD I BLESS HIM?

...BECAUSE HE ALLOWED THOUSANDS OF CHILDREN TO BE BURNT?

...AND FUELLED SIX CREMATORIA?

ELIE WIESEL, "NIGHT"

SZLAK MANN

The Messianic Age

Where some religions may refer to a golden age in the past, Judaism places all its hope in a **better future** for itself and the whole of humanity.

ACCORDING TO THE JEWISH CALENDAR THE DAY STARTS AT SUNSET ON THE EVENING: THE DARK OF THE NIGHT IS FOLLOWED BY THE LIGHT OF THE DAY.

How will we recognize the messianic age?

The Messiah will come to earth.

He shall bring everlasting peace to the world.

163

But Judaism favors neither pacifism, nor non-violence, **recognizing the right to self-defense** (very clearly defined in rabbinical literature) insisting that peace cannot be achieved at the price of grave injustice.

Apart from peace on earth the messianic age will bring an abundance of material wealth for all humanity.

ACCORDING TO JEWISH TRADITION, HUMANITY WILL REVERT TO VEGETARIANISM, AS BEFORE THE FLOOD....

When the messianic age dawns, God will end the term of exile of the Jewish people.
All Israel will make its *teshuvah* (return).

It will, in fact, be a double return:
—a **spiritual** return, i.e., repentance (see p. 49).
—also a **material** return, i.e., a return to the Holy Land.

Moreover, restoration of the State of Israel is regarded by a number of contemporary commentators as one of the precursors of the messianic age.

The whole world will ultimately recognize God and accept His sovereignty.

But when will the Messiah come?
Speculation on the subject is not recommended.

However . . .

167

There are many paths to the messianic age, and Jewish messianism has nothing to do with the idea of organized ideological imperialism.

According to tradition, the messianic age will be **preceded by a number of disasters,** comparable to "labor pains."

The messianic age will not be a supernatural one, as it is said: "In the messianic age, the universe will continue to function by the same laws."

And after the messianic age?
According to several sages, it is then that **"the dead will be resurrected."**

"THE ALMIGHTY HAS SPOKEN TO THESE BONES, SAYING: I SHALL BREATHE LIFE INTO YOU AND YOU SHALL LIVE.'"

And afterwards? See p. 36.

After the emancipation: plurality and unity of the Jewish people

With the exception of Holland, the structure of Jewish communities by the mid-18th century was generally as follows:
—**Segregation by law:** Jews were relegated to certain professions; they were mostly forced to live in segregated areas only.
—**Relative internal autonomy:** jurisdiction, administration, and education were all provided by the rabbinical authorities. With the triumph of the "age of enlightenment," and starting with the French Revolution, **the Jews were granted citizenship and equal rights** as a prelude to integration in the societies in which they lived: **this was the emancipation.**

Integration was assiduously sought by a growing faction of the Jewish world.

The conquests of the French Revolution extended this process throughout Europe. By the end of the 19th century all the Jews in Europe—except in the Russian empire—had been granted equal rights.

Henceforth Jews were free to choose their way of life, not having to submit to any rabbinical authority or any restrictive national measures in their countries of residence (except in Poland and Russia). Various schools of thought emerged, according to the response to the following:

Four great movements breaking away from orthodoxy:
—Reform
—Zionism
—Socialism
—Assimilation

The reform Movement:

Born of the desire to reconcile Judaism with the modern world, the Reform Movement, in its most extreme form, **led to the abandonment of any reference to Jewish nationalism in favor of citizenship of the country of residence** (in this way responding to the centralist ideology of the nation-state).

The idea of the citizen of the Jewish persuasion mainly developed in western Europe until 1939, with members of the Reform Movement proposing new forms of practicing Judaism: abandoning Hebrew, introducing the organ in services, and replacing the Sabbath with Sunday, etc.

Some Jewish communities—particularly in France and Germany—who were excited by this new outlook, even **adopted an exaggerated patriotism.**

174

Overall, the emancipation promoted intense cultural and scientific activity, which some historians found redolent of the more traditional schools of Jewish thought.

GRANDPA FREUD

Zionism

A definition of what is common to all factions of the Zionist movement:

—It is the ideology proclaiming that it is a **right** and **necessity** for the Jewish people to have a sovereign Jewish State in the land of Israel.

—**The right:** having been chased from their land by the Romans, the Jews are merely returning to it.

—**The necessity:** the only solution to ending anti-Semitism is to have a Jewish society with sovereign nationhood in the Jew's own land.

Born out of nationalism, Zionism propounds the idea of the Jewish nation independent of the Jewish religion.

The Zionist movement is actually at the heart of a dialectic between **a surrender to modern times versus fidelity to Jewish tradition.**

■ **But there are also aspects firmly rooted in the Jewish tradition:**

—Attachment to the land of Israel:

The Zionist movement, although largely non-religious, refused the British proposal of setting up a state in Uganda!

—Attachment to the Bible, the history of the Jewish people, and to Jewish festivals.

—An extraordinary resurgence of Hebrew as a living language.

ZIONISM SPRINGS FROM TWO SOURCES. THE FIRST BEING DEEP-ROOTED AND IRRATIONAL: THIS IS THE MESSIANIC FAITH.

(DAVID BEN GURION, FIRST PRIME MINISTER OF ISRAEL)

■ Jews and the revolutionary movement!
(The jilted lover's spite.)

The first theoreticians of "utopian socialism" (except Saint-Simon), including Marx himself, clearly proclaimed their anti-Semitism:

However, the socialist movements abandoned these positions at the end of the 19th century, after which the Jews flocked towards socialism, rapidly rising from militants to leaders. Why?

1. Under the Tsars . . .

2. In western Europe (Germany, France, Austria) hatred of the Jews became an essential part of right-wing nationalism from the mid-19th century.
The Jews therefore went in the opposite direction.

3. Also . . .

—A number of Jews thought they could see a link between the traditions of their fathers and the revolutionary message. . . .

Some of the Jewish sons and daughters of the revolution: Rosa Luxemburg, Trotsky, Zinoviev, Bela Kun, etc.

THE JEWISH INVOLVEMENT IN REVOLUTIONARY MOVEMENTS CONTINUED OVER SEVERAL GENERATIONS.

HOWEVER, RABID ANTISEMITISM AND THE SYSTEMATIC ANTI-ISRAEL POLICY OF THE USSR AND ITS ALLIES PUT AN END TO THIS GREAT ILLUSION.

The Bund (Confederation of Jewish Workers of Poland)

Founded at the end of the 19th century, this organization existed in Tsarist Russia and Poland up to 1939. It is a **specifically Jewish** movement for social democracy.

Extremely powerful in Poland until 1939, the *Bund . . .*

. . . all but disappeared in the crematoria. Today, a handful of survivors and intellectuals strive to perpetuate the memory.

But the 20th century, too, is an era of virulent anti-Semitism, though different in content and methods.

Racial anti-Semitism

In the Middle Ages, rejection of the Jews was linked to their religious convictions (i.e., it was more a form of anti-Judaism). Apart from Spain (see p. 27), conversion to Christianity was enough, in general, to guarantee security.

—With the emancipation, which granted Jews citizenship regardless of their religious convictions, a new form of anti- Semitism appeared, detachment from religion and based on "race."

From the 19th century, racial anti-Semitism became a powerful instrument of both nascent nationalism and socialism.

Thus, in the Dreyfus Affair (1894), which concerned a Jewish captain in the French army . . .

This new anti-Semitism attempted to deny the Jew the status acquired as a result of the emancipation.

But thanks to Jaurès and Zola, among others, the socialist movements abandoned anti-Semitism after the Dreyfus Affair and from then on took part in the fight against discrimination.

After this the nationalistic movements made hatred of the Jews an important element of their ideology, independent of any references to religion.

Nazism represents the culmination of all these movements:

—"left-wing" anti-Semitism—against "judeo-capitalism."
—"right-wing" anti-Semitism—against "judeo-bolshevism."
—racism and nationalism—separation of the Jewish "race" from the "Aryan" peoples.

The Nazis did in fact succeed in exterminating the major part of European Jewry, regardless of whether they were orthodox or nonpracticing, right-wing or left-wing, Zionists or advocates of assimilation, parents or children . . .

	1939	1945
POLAND	3,000,000	120,000
USSR	3,500,000	2,500,000
GERMANY	500,000	20,000
FRANCE	300,000	175,000
GREECE	75,000	7,500
ROMANIA	1,000,000	320,000
CZECHO-SLOVAKIA	360,000	40,000
YUGOSLAVIA	75,000	7,500
ETC.		

* STATISTICS TAKEN FROM CECIL ROTH: HISTORY OF THE JEWISH PEOPLE (1980).

Only the Jews of Denmark and Bulgaria were saved, thanks to the courage of these two nations.

Soviet anti-Semitism

The Soviet state, since Stalin, is one of the few countries to have a policy of anti-Semitism:

—prohibition of emigration to Israel,
—prohibition of the teaching of Hebrew and Jewish traditions,
—a quota system in universities and in professions,
—anti-Semitic press campaigns.

The Arab—Israeli conflict

Essentially of a political nature, this conflict does not have the uncompromising character of the fight against anti-Semitism (as the peace between Egypt and Israel has demonstrated). However, some Arab states (Syria in particular) still persist in persecuting the handful of Jews remaining. The terrorist organizations have certainly not shrunk from attacking synagogues and assassinating Jews anywhere in the world, thus revealing their deep-rooted hatred of Jews.

And today?

The Jewish world has changed profoundly.
Its geographical distribution has shifted:
The two major Jewish centers of the world are the U.S. and Israel.

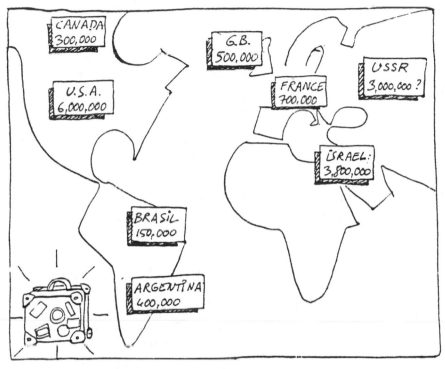

—In the space of a few years (an acceleration of history?) the Jews experienced the two most traumatic events since the start of the great exile:

—the Holocaust (the genocide of one-third of the Jewish people).

> ... WHICH SHATTERED ILLUSIONS ENTERTAINED SINCE THE EMANCIPATION.

—the creation of the State of Israel.

> ... WHICH OVERTURNED THE SITUATION OF THE JEWS, GIVING THEM RENEWED CONFIDENCE IN THE FUTURE.

There are still many ways of being Jewish . . .

. . . but they do not dilute the strong sense of unity: nity:

And now it appears that there is a return to Jewish tradition in all its forms:

Bibliography

Fundamental Texts:
Holy Bible: King James Text. Modern Phrased Version, New York, Oxford University Press, 1980.

Maimonides, Moses, *The Guide of the Perplexed*, trans. S. Pines, Chicago, University of Chicago Press, 1963.

The Prophets, Philadelphia, The Jewish Publication Society of America, 1978.

The Torah: New English Version of the Jewish Publication Society and A Modern Commentary, New York, Union of Hebrew Congregations, 1981.

The Writings-Kethubim: A New Translation of The Holy Scriptures According to the Masoretic Text. Third Section, Philadelphia, The Jewish Publication Society of America, 1982.

General Books:
Encyclopaedia Judaica, 16 vols, Jerusalem, Keter Publishing House Ltd., 1971–2.

Adam, Charles J. (ed.), *A Reader's Guide to the Great Religions*, 2nd edition, New York, The Free Press, 1977.

Jewish History and Literature:
Baron, Salo Wittmayer, *A Social and Religious History of the Jews*, 2nd edition, New York, Columbia University Press, 1952–76.

Ben-Sasson, H. H. (ed.), *A History of the Jewish People*, London, Weidenfeld and Nicolson Ltd., 1976.

Laqueur, Walter, *A History of Zionism*, New York, Schocken Books, Inc., 1976.

Roth, Cecil, *A Short History of the Jewish People*, revised and enlarged edition, London, East and West Library, 1969.

Sachar, Howard Morley, *The Course of Modern Jewish History*, updated and expanded edition, New York, Dell, 1977.

—— *A History of Israel*, New York, Alfred A. Knopf, Inc., 1976.

Seltzer, Robert M., *Jewish People, Jewish Thought: The Jewish Experience in History*, New York, Macmillan Publishing Co.; London, Collier Macmillan Publishers, 1980.

Zinberg, Israel, *A History of Jewish Literature*, trans. B. Martin, 12 vols. Vols. 1–3, Cleveland, Ohio, Case Western Reserve, 1972–73. Vols. 4–12, New York, Ktav Publishing House, 1974–78.

Jewish Religion:
Cohen, A., *Everyman's Talmud*, New York, Schocken Books, Inc., 1975.

Jacobs, Louis, *A Jewish Theology*, New York, Behrman House, Inc., 1973.

Neusner, Jacob, *Invitation to the Talmud: A Teaching Book*, New York, Harper & Row, Publishers, 1973.

—— *The Way of Torah: An Introduction to Judaism*, 2nd edition, Encino, Calif., Dickenson Publishing Co., Inc., 1974.

Schechter, Solomon, *Studies in Judaism: A Selection*, Philadelphia, The Jewish Publication Society of America, 1958.

Jewish Philosophy:

Blau, Joseph L., *The Story of Jewish Philosophy*, New York, Random House, Inc., 1962.

Fackenheim, Emil L., *The Jewish Return to History: Reflections in the Age of Auschwitz and a New Jerusalem*, New York, Schocken Books, Inc., 1978.

Glatzer, Nahum N. (ed.), *Studies in Jewish Thought*, Philadelphia, The Jewish Publication Society of America, 1974.

Guttmann, Julius, *Philosophies of Judaism: The History of Jewish Philosophy from Biblical Times to Franz Rosenzweig*, trans. D. W. Silverman, New York, Holt, Rinehart and Winston, 1964.

Jospe, Alfred (ed. and trans.), *Jerusalem and Other Jewish Writings*, New York, Schocken Books, Inc., 1969.

Katz, Steven T. (ed.), *Jewish Philosophers*, New York, Bloch Publishing Co., Inc., 1975.

Scholem, Gershom, *On Jews and Judaism in Crisis: Selected Essays*, New York, Schocken Books, Inc., 1976.

Wiesel, Elie, *A Jew Today*, trans. from the French by Marion Wiesel, New York, Random House, Inc., 1978.

Jewish Mysticism and Kabbalah:

Jacobs, Louis (ed.), *Jewish Ethics, Philosophy, and Mysticism*, New York, Behrman House, 1969.

Scholem, Gershom, *Major Trends in Jewish Mysticism*, 3rd edition, New York, Schocken Books, Inc., 1954.

—— *On the Kabbalah and Its Symbolism*, trans. R. Manheim, New York, Schocken Books, Inc., 1965.

—— (ed.), *Zohar: The Book of Splendor*, New York, Schocken Books, Inc., 1963.